Cats Rule!

Snap books®

Favorite CAT BREEDS

Persians, Abyssinians, Siamese, Sphynx, and all the Breeds In-Between

by Angie Peterson Kaelberer

CAPSTONE PRESS
a capstone imprint

Snap Books are published by Capstone
1710 Roe Crest Drive, North Mankato, Minnesota 56003
www.mycapstone.com

Library of Congress Cataloging-in-Publication Data
Cataloging-in-Publication data is on file with the Library of Congress.
ISBN 978-1-4914-8402-9 (library binding)
ISBN 978-1-4914-8414-2 (eBook PDF)

Editorial Credits
Carrie Sheely and Alesha Halvorson, editors
Philippa Jenkins, designer
Svetlana Zhurkin, media researcher
Steve Walker, production specialist

Printed and bound in US

We would like to thank Laurie Patton, Regional Director, TICA Southeast, for her invaluable help in the preparation of this book.

Photo Credits
Capstone Press: Philippa Jenkins, back cover and throughout; Dreamstime: Brittneygobble, 27, Linda Johnsonbaugh, 25; Getty Images: SSPL, 5; Newscom: AdMedia/Birdie Thompson, 12, Europics, 14 (top), facebook/blindcathoneybee/ZJAN, 17 (top), Zuma Press/Caters News, 20; Shutterstock: bonzodog, 15, Chris Rinckes, 19, cynoclub, 23, Daria Filimonova, 13, Dmitry Maslov, 21, Eric Isselee, cover (front and middle), 14 (bottom), Ewais, 8, 18 (bottom), Jaguar PS, 18 (top), Kirill Vorobyev, cover (left), klom, 10, Krissi Lundgren, 22, Lisa A, 29, nelik, 11, Rob Hainer, 17 (bottom), Sarah Fields Photography, 4, Vladyslav Starozhylov, 6₀

Table of Contents

CHAPTER 1

It's a Cat's World

According to an old saying, dogs are man's best friend. But that might not be as true anymore. At least 74 million pet cats live in the United States, compared to about 70 million dogs. Many pet owners prefer cats because they don't require as much space as many dog breeds. Cats also don't need to be taken outside for walks as frequently as dogs.

Cats and their owners share a special bond. If you have a tough day, your cat is there to purr, rub against your legs, cuddle on your lap, or just listen.

Cat History

Scientists believe the domestic cat probably developed around 9,000 years ago from an African wildcat known as *felis silvestris lybica*. In those times people kept cats mainly because they killed mice, rats, and other pesky rodents. Cats later moved into people's homes as pets. Cat mummies have been found in the tombs of wealthy and important ancient Egyptians dating back to 1500 BC. Ancient Egyptians admired cats. The Egyptian goddess Bastet had a cat's head and a woman's body.

As ancient people moved into new areas, they took their cats with them. By the 1400s cats reached the New World on the ships of European explorers. In North and South America, they continued to keep their owners' homes free from pests.

🐾 Cat Breeds Galore!

Cats don't have as many differences in size and physical features as dogs do. That's one reason people don't always realize there are many cat breeds. Like dogs, cat breeds are different in both appearance and personality. Cat breeds can have short hair, long hair—or almost no hair! Some breeds love to play with their owners and be involved in whatever they're doing, while others are more independent.

The earliest cat breeds are considered "natural" breeds because they came about with little or no influence from people. These breeds, which include the Persian, Siamese, Turkish Angora, Egyptian Mau, and Burmese, date back as far as 3,000 years ago. By the late 1800s, cats were popular pets in Europe. Owners began mating cats to produce kittens with certain **traits** or even to produce entirely new breeds. A cat show at London's Crystal Palace in 1871 increased the popularity of several breeds, including the Siamese, Abyssinian, and British Shorthair.

Today nearly 100 cat breeds exist. About half of them are recognized by cat breed associations. These breeds can compete for breed championship awards in cat shows. Cat breed associations include the Cat Fanciers' Association (CFA) and The International Cat Association (TICA).

Most popular breeds, Cat Fanciers' Association	
1	Exotic
2	Persian
3	Maine Coon
4	Ragdoll
5	British Shorthair
6	American Shorthair
7	Abyssinian
8	Sphynx
9	Siamese
10	Scottish Fold

Most popular breeds, The International Cat Association	
1	Bengal
2	Ragdoll
3	Maine Coon
4	Persian
5	Sphynx
6	Siamese
7	Himalayan
8	Siberian
9	Norwegian Forest
10	Abyssinian

trait—a quality or characteristic that makes one person or animal different from another

CHAPTER 2

Shorthaired Breeds

It's a fact of life—dealing with cat hair on your clothes and furniture is part of owning a cat. But short cat hairs are usually easier to clean up than long cat hairs. Shorthaired breeds also don't need daily brushing and combing. If you're looking for a more low-maintenance cat, a shorthair is probably a good bet.

British Shorthair

Ever heard of a cat invasion? The British Shorthair may be descended from cats that traveled to the United Kingdom with Roman invaders about 2,000 years ago.

The British Shorthair is a sturdy cat with a large, round head and wide eyes. Their coats can be almost any color or pattern, from solid to tricolor to tabby. British Shorthairs are known for their calm, quiet personalities. They are affectionate but don't demand attention from their owners.

Because they are mellow and quiet, British Shorthair cats are great family pets..

Colorful Cats

Cats come in many colors and patterns. Even a single litter of kittens can come in multiple colors. The three most common color patterns are solid, tabby, and pointed, although different breeds may have different color standards.

Cat Colors and Patterns		
solid	one color throughout	
bi-color	white and one color	
colorpoint	light-colored coats with a darker color or pattern on the face, ears, legs, and tail	
tabby	lighter main color with darker stripes or spots	
calico	patches of two or more colors, such as black, tan, or orange	
tortoiseshell	black with patches of orange	
ticked	each hair has alternating light and dark bands	
van	white coat with a colored tail and splashes of color between the ears	

🐾 American Shorthair

These cats go all the way back to the New World's first colonists. The breed began with British Shorthair cats that came from Europe with some of the New World's first colonists in the early 1600s. Breeders chose beautiful cats with good personalities and certain colors to create a new breed. In 1966 the breed was renamed the American Shorthair.

American Shorthairs are similar in looks and personality to their British cousins. Their coats come in nearly every color or pattern, with the silver, or gray tabby, being one of the most common.

Did You Know?

What if all blondes were girls and all redheads were boys? Something like that happens in the cat world. Nearly all calico and tortoiseshell cats are female, and most red or orange tabbies are male.

American Shorthair cats are gentle companions.

10

Abyssinians love to
play and have
a lot of energy.

🐾 Abyssinian

Those who prefer dogs to cats will probably get along well with the Abyssinian. Abys are outgoing and like being involved in whatever their owners are doing. Instead of being shy with strangers, they'll run to the door to greet visitors. Many even enjoy playing games of fetch! They love to climb and their energy level remains high after they grow into adulthood. If you want a cat that snoozes in the sunshine all day, an Aby probably isn't for you.

People often remark that Abys look like little cougars. Their coats are ticked. Each hair has bands of light and dark hair, similar to wildcat coats. Their bodies are long and slender. Coat colors include ruddy (brown), red (orange), blue (gray), and fawn (beige).

Abyssinians got their name from the country of Abyssinia, which today is called Ethiopia. But no one is sure if the cats' ancestors actually came from Ethiopia. Most cat experts believe the breed began in the late 1800s in Great Britain. In 1871 Abys were part of the first cat show at the Crystal Palace in London.

LIL BUB

Lil Bub is a tiny brown tabby adopted from an animal shelter. She is famous for her kittenlike appearance, even though she's an adult. Lil Bub was the smallest in her litter and had to be bottle-fed. Her tongue sticks out because she has a shorter lower jaw. She also has a bone disorder that caused her growth to be stunted.

 ## Siamese

Would you like to have a conversation with your cat? If so, the Siamese is the breed for you! They are one of the most vocal breeds. If you speak to a Siamese, it's likely to reply with a loud "meow."

The Siamese is one of the oldest cat breeds. It began in Thailand, which was once called Siam. In the early 1870s, the rest of the world got to know Siamese cats when they were part of a cat show in London.

Siamese are famous for their light-colored coats with darker fur on the tail, feet, and ears. These darker areas are called points. Point colors include seal (dark brown), chocolate (medium brown), blue (dark gray), and lilac (pale gray).

The Siamese is one of the most outgoing breeds. They don't like to spend a lot of time alone. If you're not able to be home most of the day, you'll want to get another pet as a friend for your Siamese.

Seal Point Siamese cats have very dark points on their faces, ears, tails, and paws.

Did You Know?

All Siamese kittens are born with white coats. The points appear in a few weeks and reach full color in a few months. Siamese carry a **gene** that is sensitive to heat. The body parts where the point colors appear are cooler than the rest of the body. A Siamese in a cooler climate will have darker points than one in a warmer climate.

gene—a part of every cell that carries physical and behavioral information passed from parents to their children

SNOOPY

Snoopy is an Exotic from China. His plush coat and wide eyes make him look like a stuffed toy. His owner posts many photos of him on the Internet, usually wearing bandannas, neckties, and other cute accessories.

🐾 Exotic

The Exotic is an American breed. It began in the 1960s when breeders mated longhaired Persians with American Shorthairs, Burmese, and Russian Blues. These breeders wanted a cat with the Persian's appearance and personality, but a shorter coat. The Exotic's face is similar to a Persian, but it has a plush, short coat that's easier to groom.

An Exotic has a sturdy body, short legs, and a round head. Its large, round eyes give it a sweet look. Its soft coat can be any color or pattern.

If you want a cuddly cat, an Exotic is a great choice. Its nickname is the "teddy bear cat." Exotics love to curl up in their owner's lap for a nap or to be petted.

Did You Know?

In 2014 the Exotic became the CFA's number one cat breed. It took over the top spot from the Persian, which had held it since the 1970s.

Exotic cats love the company of others, including other pets.

14

🐾 Sphynx

Maybe you don't want to deal with cat hair at all. In that case, the Sphynx could be your perfect pet.

Sphynx are known as hairless cats, but their bodies are usually covered with a light **down** that's difficult to see. Their skin feels soft and can be a number of different colors and patterns. They have rounded bodies and large ears.

The breed began as a genetic **mutation** with several hairless kittens born in the 1960s and 1970s. Those cats and their offspring were crossed with Devon Rex cats, which have very short hair, to create the Sphynx.

Because of their lack of thick fur, Sphynx get cold and sunburned easily. And even though they don't shed, their bodies still need care. Their skin produces oil, so they need to be bathed occasionally and wiped daily with a soft, damp cloth.

down—soft, light hair on a person or animal
mutataion—a natural, unexpected change in a gene

CHAPTER 3

Longhaired Breeds

Many people find longhaired cats especially attractive. However, most longhaired breeds need to be combed or brushed daily to keep their long hair from forming **mats**.

🐾 Himalayan

What do you get when you cross a Persian with a Siamese? A Himalayan! This cat has the long, silky coat of a Persian with the blue eyes and point markings of a Siamese.

Himalayans, or Himmies for short, have been described as combining the best features of both breeds. They are more active than Persians but quieter and calmer than the typical Siamese.

Did You Know?

The Birman cat looks much like the Himalayan. However, it has four white paws and its body is longer and less compact than that of the Himalayan or Persian. The Birman's coat also isn't as thick, so it's easier to groom.

mat—a thick, tangled mass of hair

HONEY BEE

Honey Bee is a blind calico cat from Seattle. As a kitten, Honey Bee had a painful eye condition that resulted in the loss of both eyes. Although Honey Bee can't see, she goes on hikes with her family. She walks on a leash and is famous for riding on her owners' backpack.

Himmies are affectionate pets.

GRUMPY CAT

TV and social media star Grumpy Cat's real name is Tardar Sauce. Her owner says she's not really grumpy—her expression comes from the fact that she's a **dwarf** cat. Her markings are similar to a Himalayan or Ragdoll, but her parents were a calico and a gray tabby.

 Persian

The Persian's sweet expression, soft coat, and gentle personality have made it a popular breed since the late 1800s. Until 2014 it was the CFA's most popular breed for more than 30 years.

Like Exotics, Persians have sturdy bodies, short legs, round heads, and large eyes. However, their coats are long and flowing. Long fur around the Persian's neck forms a **ruff** that looks something like a lion's mane. The ruff, along with the underbelly and tail, need extra grooming to keep them free of mats.

Persians are among the quietest cats. When they do meow, it's soft and low. They're affectionate and love to cuddle.

Persians have sweet and gentle personalities.

Ragdolls are laid-back and well-behaved pets.

 # Ragdoll

The Ragdoll breed began in the 1960s in the United States. Its name comes from its tendency to completely relax when picked up—becoming as soft and limp as a ragdoll. The Ragdoll enjoys being around people. Its gentle, affectionate personality makes it a good pet for families with children.

Ragdolls are one of the largest cat breeds and can weigh more than 20 pounds (9 kilograms). They grow slower than most cat breeds, reaching their full size at about age 4.

Many Ragdolls have point markings. Some are mitted, meaning they have white front paws and white back legs up to the knee. Others have bi-color patterns. While their hair is long, it doesn't tangle easily. Two or three brushings each week is enough.

dwarf—a very small person, animal, or plant
ruff—a ring of long hair around an animal's neck

🐾 Maine Coon

This breed developed naturally in the eastern United States in the 1800s. No one is sure of the breed's history, but longhaired cats that traveled on ships from Europe may have mated with shorthaired cats already living in the area.

The Maine Coon is the official state cat breed of Maine. These large cats get their name from the state and also from their long, fluffy tails, which look much like those of raccoons.

Maine Coons are long and muscular. They can weigh as much as 20 pounds (9 kg). But these gentle giants' meows sound more like a chirp. They are outgoing and playful.

Maine Coons can be almost any color or pattern, with tabby being the most common. Their coats have two layers. The outer layer helps repel water and the inner layer keeps the cat's body warm. The fur doesn't mat easily and needs only an occasional combing.

MARU

Maru is a Scottish Fold from Japan. He's the star of many Internet videos. He often tries to squeeze or jump into a small box.

A fluffy Maine Coon's coat is silky but oily.

CHAPTER 4
New and Unique

Serengeti

Are you ready to walk on the wild side? Most new breeds are created from two or more established breeds. But some breeders go back to the domestic cat's wild cousins to develop new breeds. These **hybrid** breeds are a much-debated issue in the cat world. Many people say that wildcat traits and behavior don't belong in a house pet. Others like the hybrids' unique appearance and high energy.

Serengeti

If you like the look of a wildcat, then the Serengeti may be for you. This cat has a spotted coat, long legs, and large ears like a wildcat does. But it is smaller and has a mellower personality more suited for a home.

The Serengeti began in the 1990s when breeders crossed Oriental cats with Bengals. They created an outgoing cat that likes to climb. Like Siamese, the Serengeti is vocal and will hold its own in a "conversation."

hybrid—a plant or animal that has been bred from two different species or varieties

The most popular Bengal color is a brown and black tabby.

Bengal

The Bengal began in the 1960s when scientist Jean S. Mill crossed a domestic cat with a small wildcat called an Asian leopard cat. The wildcat is immune to **feline leukemia**. Mill and her colleague Dr. Willard Centerwall hoped to produce a cat that would also be immune to the disease. That didn't happen, but other breeders continued her work. They crossed the Asian Leopard Cat with popular domestic cats, such as British and American Shorthairs, Bombays, and Egyptian Maus. By the 1980s the Bengal was an established breed.

Bengals are large and muscular, weighing up to 15 pounds (7 kg). Their coats are a mixture of spotted and tabby markings. These energetic cats need lots of playtime with their owners. Otherwise, curtains and treasured keepsakes can turn into Bengal toys. Even a Bengal with wildcats as distant descendants will show behaviors that don't always fit into a regular home.

feline leukemia—a disease of cats caused by a virus; feline leukemia causes weight loss, infections, and eventually death

Savannah

Probably the hybrid closest to its wild roots, the Savannah is one of the newest cat breeds. It began in 1986 when a breeder crossed a domestic female Siamese with a male serval. The cat had one kitten, which the breeder named Savannah, after the African grasslands where the serval lives.

The Savannah gets its spotted coat, large ears, and hooded eyes from its serval ancestors. It loves to climb, and its long legs help it leap up to 8 feet (2.5 meters). Unlike many breeds, the Savannah often enjoys playing in water.

Like Bengals, Savannahs are social cats and need lots of playtime. Savannah owners should "cat-proof" their homes by putting away breakable objects and covering electrical cords. Savannahs are intelligent, and many figure out how to turn on faucets or open cabinets and drawers. Changing the taps and installing childproof latches on cabinets will help solve this problem.

generation—all the members of a group of people or animals born around the same time
serval—a long-legged African wildcat with a spotted coat

Savannahs are known for their jumping abilities.

Lykoi

Do you like scary movies? Then you just might like the look of one of the newest cat breeds, the Lykoi. Its rough coat and hairless patches make it look like a werewolf!

The Lykoi isn't a hybrid. It's a domestic cat with a recessive gene. Some **feral** cats produced kittens that were born solid black but soon lost hair on areas of their bodies. The remaining fur turned to a mixture of black and white hairs. Other kittens were born without any hair at all. Breeders had the kittens tested to make sure the hairlessness wasn't caused by a disease. Then they began breeding them with black cats to produce the Lykoi.

The Lykoi has little to no hair on the back of its ears or around the eyes, chin, or nose. Most have little hair on their legs and feet. They have intelligent personalities, similiar to wolves. They enjoy "hunting" for toys and will play games of fetch. Lykois don't warm up quickly to new people or animals. But once you win their trust, they are very protective.

feral—to do with or like wild animals

A Lykoi may shed its hair and then regrow it later in its ife.

Which Cat Breed is Best for You?

Choosing a Cat

Small or large. Shorthaired or long. Friendly or independent. All of these characteristics and more are found in our feline friends. Doing a little homework on what you and your family want in a cat will help you find the breed that's the purr-fect match!

1 **What is your home like?**

   a. My mom has a million glass decorations all over.
   b. Our house is uncluttered and simple.
   c. My family can't stand dust anywhere!

2 **How do you want to spend time with your pet?**

   a. I could cuddle with my cat 24/7.
   b. I want to play fetch and other games with my cat every day.
   c. I would love my pets, but I have lots of activities I'm involved in.

3 **How do you feel about grooming your cat?**

   a. I would like brushing my cat every day—it's a great way to bond.
   b. My hair care routine is low maintenance—I want the same for my cat.
   c. I don't want to brush my cat—ever.

4 **Does anyone in your family have allergies to animals?**

   a. No, not at all.
   b. A little sneezing once in a while, but nothing too serious.
   c. Yes—major allergies to anything with fur!

Mostly A's: Your perfect cat is a Persian, Ragdoll, or Himalayan.
Mostly B's: Your perfect cat is a Siamese, Abyssinian, or Bengal.
Mostly C's: Your perfect cat is a Sphynx.

Answers

CATERING TO YOUR CAT

Cat Grass Garden

Many cats love to snack on grass. But for safety reasons, cats should be kept indoors. And even if you go outside with your cat, the grass on your lawn may not be safe for your cat to eat because of chemicals used to kill weeds. Don't worry, though—you can grow your own cat grass!

What You Need:
- medium-size flowerpot with a drainage saucer
- black dirt or organic soil
- 1 package cat grass seeds, available at most garden centers
- small watering can filled with water

What You Do:

1. Fill the flowerpot about ¾ full with dirt.

2. Use your fingers to poke five to seven holes in the dirt

3. Sprinkle about five seeds in each hole.

4. Cover the holes with about ¼ inch (6.4 millimeters) of dirt.

5. Water the pot lightly, and place it in a sunny window. Keep the soil moist. The seeds should sprout within one to two weeks. When the grass grows to a few inches tall, it's ready for your cat to munch!

Glossary

down (DOWN)—soft, light hair on a person or animal

dwarf (DWORF)—a very small person, animal, or plant

feline leukemia (FEE-line loo-KEE-mee-uh)—a disease of cats caused by a virus; feline leukemia causes weight loss, infections, and eventually death

feral (FIHR-uhl)—to do with or like wild animals

gene (JEEN)—a part of every cell that carries physical and behavioral information passed from parents to their children

generation (jen-uh-RAY-shuhn)—all the members of a group of people or animals born around the same time

hybrid (HYE-brid)—a plant or animal that has been bred from two different species or varieties

mat (MAT)—a thick, tangled mass of hair

mutation (myoo-TAY-shuhn)—a natural, unexpected change in a gene

ruff (RUHF)—a ring of long hair around an animal's neck

serval (SUHR-vuhl)—a long-legged African wildcat with a spotted coat

trait (TRATE)—a quality or characteristic that makes one person or animal different from another

Read More

Guillain, Charlotte. *Cats*. Animal Family Albums. Chicago: Raintree, 2013.

Heneghan, Judith. *Love Your Cat*. Your Perfect Pet. New York: Windmill Books, 2013.

Jeffrey, Laura S. *Choosing a Cat: How to Choose and Care for a Cat*. Pet Care Series. Berkeley Heights, N.J.: Enslow Publishers, 2013.

Thomas, Isabel. *Cool Cat Projects*. Pet Projects. Chicago: Raintree, 2016.

🐾 Internet Sites

FactHound offers a safe, fun way to find Internet sites related to this book. All of the sites on FactHound have been researched by our staff.

Here's all you do:

Visit *www.facthound.com*

Type in this code: 9781491484029

Super-cool stuff! Check out projects, games and lots more at **www.capstonekids.com**

Critical Thinking Using the Common Core

1. How are domestic cats and wildcats similar? Which breeds share the most in common with wildcats? (Key Ideas and Details)

2. Why did people tame cats? Did the relationship between cats and people benefit one or the other more, or did both benefit equally? (Integration of Knowledge and Ideas)

3. Some cat breed characteristics and traits are developed naturally. Others come from people's actions through breeding cats. Which do you think is better for the cat? Why? (Craft and Structure)

Index